THE STORY OF THE
LONDON
BRIDGE

by Alice Cary
illustrated by Jack Crane

MODERN CURRICULUM PRESS
Pearson Learning Group

London Bridge is one of the most famous bridges in the world. Millions of people have crossed it, including kings, queens, princes, and princesses. Children love to sing the Mother Goose rhyme about it falling down.

Did you know that for hundreds of years, London Bridge really *was* falling down? Now it is finally strong and sturdy. But it isn't in London anymore! It isn't even in England.

This is the story of how London Bridge began and how it changed. It is also the story of how, centuries later, it crossed the sea to begin life in another land.

The Thames (TEHMZ) is England's main river. It starts in the English countryside, flows east through London, and empties into the North Sea. Tides sweep back from the ocean, changing the river's water levels every twelve hours.

At first the Thames River had no bridge at all. There wasn't even a city named London.

The Romans founded London almost two thousand years ago. The Romans were great bridge builders who understood the concepts needed to build such structures. Some of their ideas are still used today.

The Romans may have built bridges across the Thames, or they may have used ferry boats to cross it.

Over the years, London grew bigger and bigger. Wooden bridges were probably built, but they didn't last long. They either burned or wore away.

Historians know that around the year 1000 a long wooden bridge was built over the Thames. The next year the Danish invaded. The Danes sailed close to the bridge and tied ropes to its supports. Then they sailed away and tore down the whole bridge.

Like the changing tides, London's earliest bridges came and went.

MAP OF THE BRITISH ISLES
England with Scotland and Ireland
shewing the
COUNTIES RAIL ROADS & CHANNELS.

5

In the 1100s, a man named Peter Colechurch decided the Thames needed a bridge that would last. He felt that stone would be the most durable material.

Mr. Colechurch told many people about his idea and collected money to help pay for the project.

Work began, but progress was very slow. The builders made a series of stone arches. Each arch took about eighteen months to complete. The work continued for thirty-four years!

By the time the bridge was finished in 1209, about 250 workers had been killed on the job. Peter Colechurch had also died. He was buried in a chapel built on top of the bridge.

London Bridge was finally built, but it wasn't very pretty. The construction had been haphazard, not carefully planned and executed. No two pillars were the same size. There were nineteen arches of all different sizes. Some were only fifteen-feet wide, some were thirty-five feet wide.

While London Bridge may not have been beautiful, it was practical. And it lasted six hundred years! For hundreds of years, it was London's only bridge across the Thames.

Londoners loved being able to stroll across the bridge. Down below, however, people on the river cursed the new structure.

Many of the openings between arches were small. Not only were they narrow, but some left only five feet of head space at high tide. Large boats couldn't fit underneath.

To make matters worse, water rushed under the bridge quickly. The strong current was dangerous and many boats capsized. Steering under London Bridge was called "shooting the bridge."

Londoners quickly thought up a saying. "London Bridge is made for wise men to go over," they said, "and fools to go under."

The problem was so bad that many people got off their boats before they got to the bridge. They walked onshore until they passed the bridge. Then they got into a second boat.

One duke who wasn't so lucky collided with the bridge. He leaped off his boat and grabbed the bridge, hanging on for dear life. He was hauled to safety with a rope.

There was plenty of excitement on top of London Bridge as well. Sometimes tragic things happened.

Just a few years after the bridge was built, a big fire broke out in the area. People rushed onto the bridge to watch.

Somehow fire broke out on both ends of the bridge. People were caught in the middle—between the flames. They jumped into the Thames to escape, but many died.

London Bridge became a bustling place. In fact, people built houses right on top. Not only was there a chapel and a drawbridge, but as many as one hundred houses were built on it. Often merchants had shops downstairs and lived upstairs.

One four-story house was especially fancy. It was brought over in pieces from Holland. Instead of using nails, workers fastened the pieces together with wooden pegs.

The building became known as "Nonesuch House." That's because people had seen none such a house like this before.

Eventually the bridge became so crowded that there was scarcely room for people to walk on it. There were so many buildings that the Thames could barely be seen. It could be spotted from only three places along the way.

Still, kings and queens passed over countless times. There were royal celebrations and royal funerals.

Occasionally, though, the crowds turned wild. Once in 1263, for example, people who did not like the new queen, Eleanor, threw things at her, including rocks, as she began to "shoot the bridge" aboard the royal barge. But she wasn't hurt.

There was a house on London Bridge that belonged to a rich cloth maker named William Hewett. One day a nurse in his employ was looking out the window as she held his baby. Something caught her attention and she leaned out farther. Suddenly she dropped the baby into the rushing water below! For an instant the child disappeared in the rapids.

A quick-thinking boy named Edward, who had seen the accident, jumped into the Thames and rescued the baby. Years later, when the baby girl had grown up, she and Edward were married.

As the years passed, the bridge began to fall apart. But troubles had started early. About seventy years after the bridge was built, an accumulation of heavy winter ice caused five of the bridge's arches to collapse.

Tolls were collected to help pay for bridge repairs, but there still wasn't enough money to fix the bridge properly. Things got so bad that at least one house fell into the water.

In 1666 another fire broke out. This one was so big that it was called the Great Fire of London. This time the flames didn't spread across the bridge. However, areas near the bridge were ruined.

By the eighteenth century, shops and homes on the bridge had turned from fancy to shabby. London Bridge was truly falling down.

By this time, new bridges were being built across the Thames. Londoners decided it was finally time to fix London Bridge.

England's expert on bridges was a man named John Rennie. In the 1820s, he was asked to help decide what should be done about the famous bridge.

Rennie walked back and forth across the bridge. He inspected it from every angle. He traveled under the bridge by boat. He climbed up and down its piers.

Rennie carefully thought about the bridge's problems. He had detected many serious flaws. He thought about the many important bridge-building concepts.

Rennie decided the bridge was beyond repair. The city would have to build a new London Bridge.

Rennie came up with a new design. So did about thirty other designers. But city officials thought Rennie's plans were best.

Rennie was sixty-one years old and in poor health. Sadly, he died before the work began. Like Peter Colechurch, who died before the original bridge was finished, Rennie never got to see his vision completed. But Rennie had taught his son, John, everything he knew about bridges so John could take over his work.

Construction began in 1823. It kept about eight hundred workers busy for seven and a half years.

The new bridge opened in 1831, only one hundred feet away from the old one, which had been torn down. Made of granite, it was very strong and beautiful. The New London Bridge had five graceful stone arches, all the same size.

Everyone loved the New London Bridge. Tourists from all over the world admired it. First, horse-drawn carriages passed over it. Later cars began to roll across.

But even national treasures become outdated. The heavy traffic became too great for the bridge. It started to slowly sink into the Thames River. About one-eighth of an inch disappeared each year.

This may seem like a tiny amount, but it worried officials. By 1968, a foot and a half had settled into the river.

Officials decided the bridge needed to be taken down. Then it would be thrown away or sold. They agreed to try selling it first. The New London Bridge would be the biggest antique ever sold—if a buyer could be found.

Meanwhile, across the Atlantic Ocean, a new city had been born in the United States.

Lake Havasu City, Arizona, began in 1938. Its large lake was formed when Parker Dam was built that year.

The city grew after a man named Robert McCulloch began testing motors there. Before long more businesses and people settled there.

McCulloch heard that London Bridge was for sale. What fun, he thought. That's just what the beaches of Lake Havasu need.

How much does a famous, old bridge cost?

McCulloch figured Londoners would have to pay $1.2 million to buy enough granite to build a replacement bridge. He decided that twice that amount, or $2.4 million, would be a fair price.

But what if someone else had the same idea? To help make sure he won the bid, McCulloch added another $60,000 to his price.

Why $60,000? McCulloch would be sixty years old by the time the bridge opened in Arizona. He added $1,000 for every year of his life.

McCulloch offered the highest price, and his offer was accepted. McCulloch's final bid was almost $2.5 million.

Others also made bids. But they had very different plans—simply to sell pieces as souvenirs. No one else had planned to rebuild the whole bridge.

Like Peter Colechurch and John Rennie before him, here was another man who dreamed about London Bridge. His was the wildest dream of all. How could he make it happen?

Taking apart a bridge, shipping it across the ocean, and rebuilding it would be a giant job. That part of the project ended up costing more than $5.5 million.

As London Bridge was taken apart in England, each stone was marked with four numbers. One number told which span it belonged to. Another number noted in which row it belonged. The final two numbers indicated the stone's position in that row.

Interestingly enough, workers discovered that the stones already had numbers. Rennie must have also used a numbering system when he built the bridge.

These thousands of stones were packed and taken by boat to California. Trucks then took loads to Lake Havasu, where they were stored.

Reconstruction began in 1968. A British engineer was in charge. He used copies of Rennie's plans as a guideline.

By 1971, his work was done. With the help of modern equipment, only forty workers did the job. London Bridge had a new home—in a desert!

The bridge was dedicated on October 10, 1971. Forty thousand people came to watch. They were treated to bands, floats, skydivers, and more.

The lord mayor of London came. He and other British officials wore seventeenth-century clothes.

When the bridge was opened, five thousand pigeons were let loose. Thirty thousand balloons filled the sky, including one that looked like a huge British flag, five stories tall.

In all its years, the world-famous bridge had never had such a party. And with luck—and, of course, care—London Bridge may never fall down again.